THOMAS BERNHARD 3 DAYS

THOMAS BERNHARD

3 DAYS

FROM THE FILM BY
FERRY RADAX

Translated from
the German by
Laura Lindgren

Afterword by
Georg Vogt

Selected works by Thomas Bernhard
translated into English

Concrete

Correction

Extinction

Frost

Gargoyles

Gathering Evidence

The Lime Works

The Loser

Old Masters

On the Mountain

Three Novellas (Amras, Playing Watten, Walking)

The Voice Imitator

Wittgenstein's Nephew

Woodcutters

Yes

A DVD of the film *Thomas Bernhard — Three Days* with subtitles is available from Index: www.index-dvd.at.

Thomas Bernhard: Three Days, from the Film by Ferry Radax
is published by Laura Lindgren / Blast Books.
P.O. Box 51, Cooper Station
New York, NY 10276-0051

Deepest gratitude to Dr. Peter Fabjan, Ferry Radax and Felix Radax, and Georg Vogt, and to Christine Burgin, Petra Hardt, Donald Kennison, Molto Menz, Herbert Pfostl, and Nina Stren.

Design and composition by Laura Lindgren

Library of Congress Cataloging-in-Publication Data
Names: Bernhard, Thomas, author. | Lindgren, Laura, translator. |
Vogt, Georg, 1975– | Radax, Ferry, 1932–
Title: 3 days : from the film by Ferry Radax / Thomas Bernhard ;
Translated from the German by Laura Lindgren ; Afterword by Georg Vogt.
Other titles: Three days
Description: New York : Blast Books, 2016.
Identifiers: LCCN 2016004440 | ISBN 9780922233465 (alk. paper)
Subjects: LCSH: Bernhard, Thomas—Criticism and interpretation. |
Authors, Austrian—20th century—Biography.
Classification: LCC PT2662.E7 Z46 2016 | DDC 838/.91409—dc23
LC record available at http://lccn.loc.gov/2016004440

Printed in China through Asia Pacific Offset

First Edition 2016

10 9 8 7 6 5 4 3 2 1

Contents

Publisher's Note

Over the course of three days, June 5, 6, and 7 in 1970, simply sitting on a white bench in a Hamburg park, Thomas Bernhard delivered a powerful monologue for *Three Days (Drei Tage)*, filmmaker Ferry Radax's commanding film portrait of the great Austrian writer. Radax interwove the monologue with a variety of metaphorically resonant visual techniques — blacking out the screen to total darkness, suggestive of the closing of the observing eye; cuts to scenes of cameramen, lighting and recording equipment; extreme camera distance and extreme close-up. Bernhard had not yet written his autobiographical work *Gathering Evidence*, published originally in five separate volumes between 1975 and 1982, and his childhood remembrances were a revelation. This publication of Bernhard's monologue and stills from Radax's artful film allows this unique portrait of Bernhard to be savored in book form.

THOMAS BERNHARD 3 DAYS

THOMAS BERNHARD

THOMAS
BERNHARD

THOMAS
BERNHARD

DREI TAGE

Hamburg 5. Juni 1970

Three Days

Hamburg June 5, 1970

1963
FROST
1964
AMRAS
1967
VERSTÖRUNG
1967
PROSA

Ungenach

At the Timberline

Watten

Events

The Lime Works

Fifteen or sixteen years ago, nearby in Wellingsbüttel, I was pacing the floor. I was trying to memorize my lines for the academy for the role of old Chrysander in *The Young Scholar* by Lessing.

Every day was the same: I'd get up and go out to the garden. I'd recite the first line and come no further... The second day, the same; I'd get to the third, fourth, fifth line, and by 4 p.m. I had come no further. And so it remained, and I never actually got past page one.

After four weeks I left.

This comes to mind because in *The Lime Works* I can't get past this single same sentence: that is, the protagonist, Konrad, in fifteen years is still only at the first sentence of a study he has wanted to write for twenty years, which just never works out for him.

All of a sudden he sits down and, as he had dreamed or imagined he would, manages all in one sitting to write the whole study down. However, it is only a dream.

Suddenly, his wife enters the room and discovers the manuscript. And she says:

> "So, behind my back you actually have written it down? An outrage!"

She grabs the entire stack of paper from his hands and incinerates it.

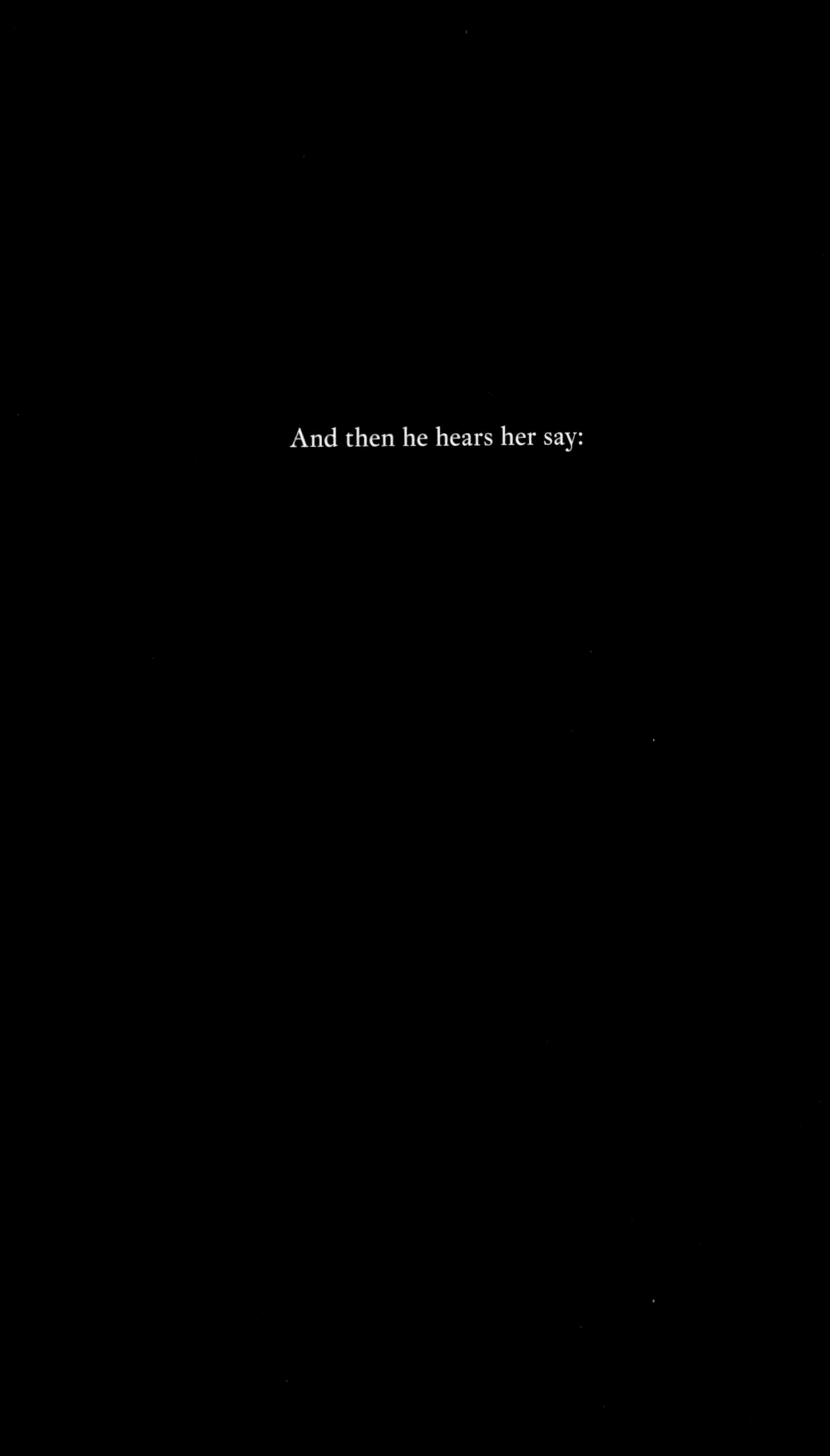
And then he hears her say:

"Now you can start all over again and struggle another twenty years with that sentence."

FIRST DAY

...First impressions—on the way to start elementary school, the first grade, passing by a butcher, doors open: rows of hatchets; hammers; knives, very neatly arranged, some of them bloody, some spick and span; stunbolt guns for slaughter.

Then the sound of a sudden slumping of horses; huge bellies that burst, collapse; bones, pus, blood...

And on past the butcher, up a few stairs to the cemetery, the mortuary, a tomb...

I remember still, from that very first school day, a pale boy laid out in the mortuary, a cheesemaker's son ...

And from there, my heart throbbing, on to school...a young school mistress...

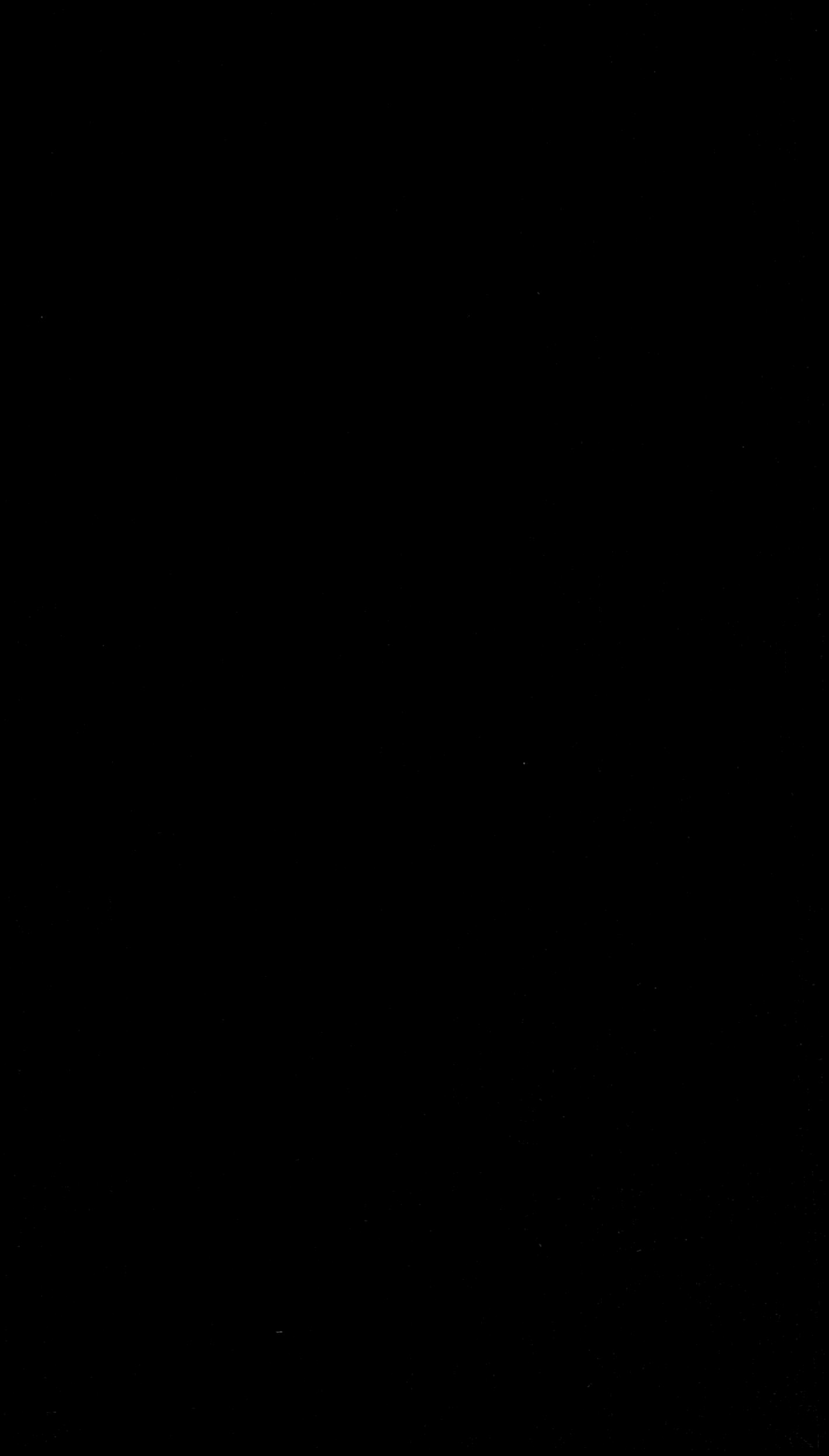

And then my grandmother, who always took me along — in the morning I passed through the cemeteries on my own; in the afternoon she took me into the mortuaries with her — would lift me up high and say,

"Look, it's a woman again."

Nothing but corpses...

And this is quite meaningful to every human being; conclusions can be drawn about everything...

Childhood — it's a repetition of musical works, although none classical. For example: in Traunstein, in 1944, the way to school was longer.

My grandparents lived outside of town, about two and a half miles away. Halfway en route to school is some shrubbery, I don't recall which kind.

And each time I pass by, a woman leaps from the bushes and shouts, "I'll take your grandfather to Dachau yet."

In 1945 another story, another piece of music, twelve-tone, perhaps. A friend of my brother's — he was seven years old then, I was fourteen — picks up a bazooka and is blown completely to bits.

The village is called Vachendorf, and I ride there by bike with my brother for the funeral.

Well, I can just barely manage to get my feet under the crossbar with my brother sitting up front on the handlebar.

Along the way we pick flowers.

But halfway to the cemetery a young man suddenly leaps from the woods, grabs my brother and me and pulls us off the bike, rips the flowers to shreds, and stomps all over the bike, completely crushing it — first he destroys the spokes, then the handlebar, then he smashes the fenders, then he slaps me, then he shoves my brother into the brook.

And it seemed to me that he was . . . I don't know exactly, was he a Pole or a Czech . . .

It was really strange. And we sat there at the edge of the brook and bawled and had to go back home on foot — continuing on to the funeral was out of the question then, and at home we told them this utterly strange story.

And there are a whole lot more like that.

Two useful lessons, of course: solitude, isolation, detachment on the one hand; on the other, perpetual mistrust — from the solitude, isolation, and detachment.

Even as a child...

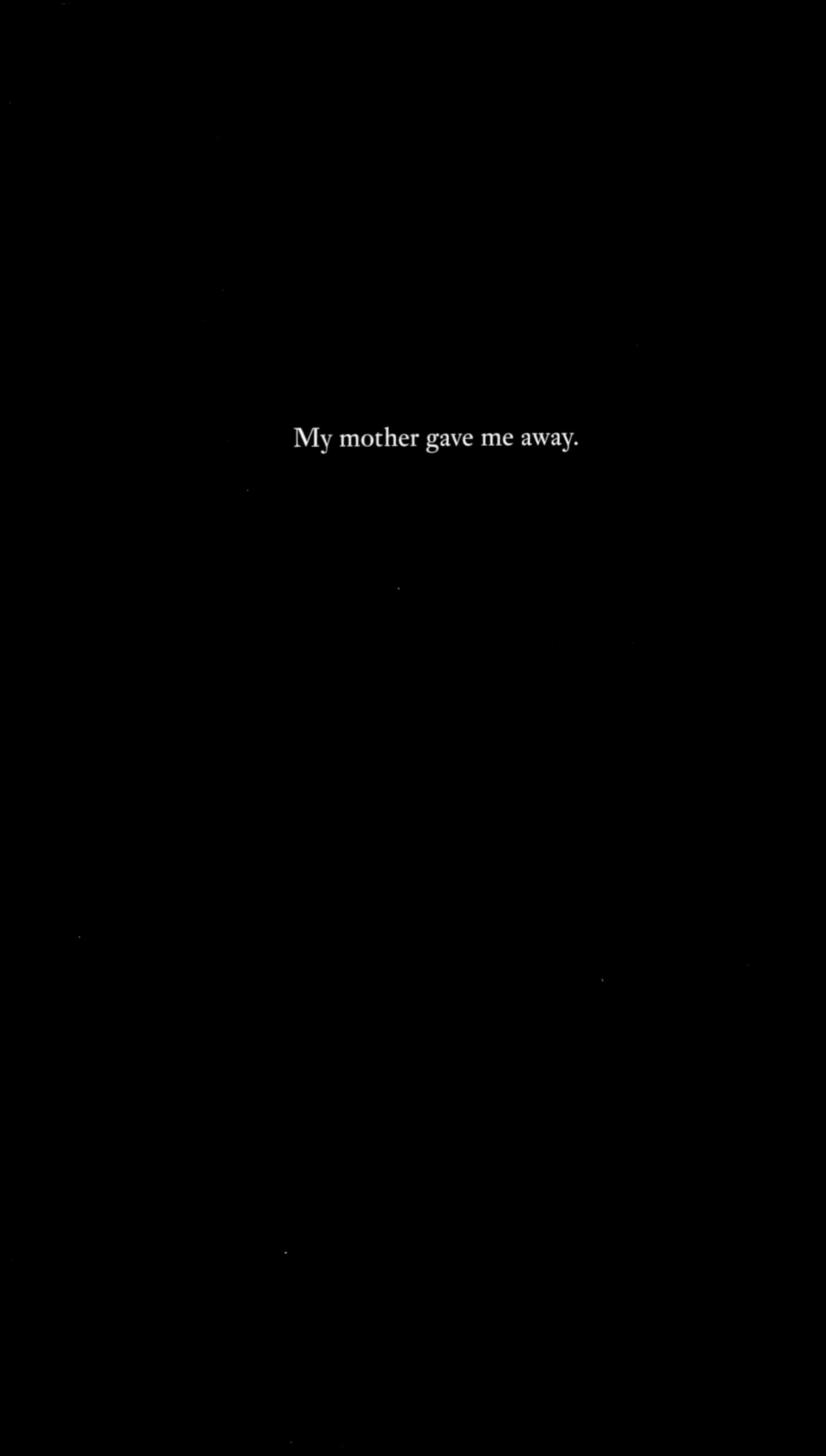
My mother gave me away.

In Holland — in Rotterdam — for a year, I was kept on a fishing trawler with a woman. My mother came to visit me there every three or four weeks. I don't think that she cared much for me at the time. However, this then changed.

I was a year old, we went to Vienna . . . and then the mistrust, lingering still when I was brought to my grandfather, who by contrast really loved me, changed.

Then taking walks with him — everything is in my books later, and all these figures, male figures, this is always my grandfather on my mother's side . . . But always — except for my grandfather — alone. Only alone can you evolve, you will always be alone . . . the consciousness that you cannot step outside of yourself.

All else is delusion, doubt. This never changes . . .

In school years completely alone.

You sit next to a schoolmate and you are alone.

You talk to people, you are alone.

You have viewpoints, differing, your own — you are always alone.

And if you write a book, or like me, books, you are yet more alone...

To make oneself understood is impossible; it cannot be done.

From loneliness and solitude comes an even more intense isolation, disconnection.

Finally you change your scenery at shorter and shorter intervals. You think, bigger and even bigger cities — the small town is no longer enough for you, not Vienna, not even London. You've got to go to some other part of the world, you try going here, there... foreign languages — maybe Brussels? Maybe Rome?

And there you go, all over the place, and you are always alone with yourself and your increasingly dreadful work.

You go back to the country, you retreat to a farmhouse, like me, you close the doors —

often days long — stay inside, and the only joy —

and at the same time ever greater pleasure — is the work. The sentences, words, you construct.

Like a toy, essentially — you stack them one atop the other; it is a musical process.

If a certain level should be reached, some four, five stories — you keep building it up — you see through the entire thing...

and like a child knock it all down. But when you think you're rid of it…

another ulcerous growth like it is already forming, an ulcer that you recognize as new work, a new novel, is bulging somewhere on your body, growing larger and larger.

In essence, isn't such a book nothing but a malignant ulcer, a cancerous tumor?

You surgically remove it knowing of course perfectly well that the metastases have already infected the entire body and that a cure is completely out of the question.

And *of course* it only gets worse and worse, and now there is no rescue, no turning back.

The people before me, my ancestors, were wonderful people. And it's no coincidence that they come to mind here on this *ice-cold* bench.

They were of every stripe: immensely rich, destitute, criminals, horrible, almost all in one way or another perverse, happy; they traveled about…

Most of them at some point suddenly committed suicide, especially those of whom it was believed that never had they had so much as a thought of putting an end to their life — or what passes for it — with a bullet or a jump. One leapt into an air shaft, another blew his brains out, and a third plunged his car into the river…

And to think of these people is as gruesome…

as it is pleasant. It is just as when you're sitting in the theater and the curtain rises,

and instantly you divide the people you see onstage into the good and the bad — and not only into good and bad *characters* or *people* and *individuals*, but into good and bad *actors*.

And I must say, to watch this performance from time to time, over and over again, is absolutely a pleasure.

SECOND DAY

The difficulty is to begin.

For the numbskull this presents no difficulty; he knows no difficulty.

He makes children or makes books, he makes *one* child, *one* book — constantly children and books.

It's all the same to him; he just doesn't think.

The numbskull knows no difficulty: he gets up, bathes, goes out on the street...

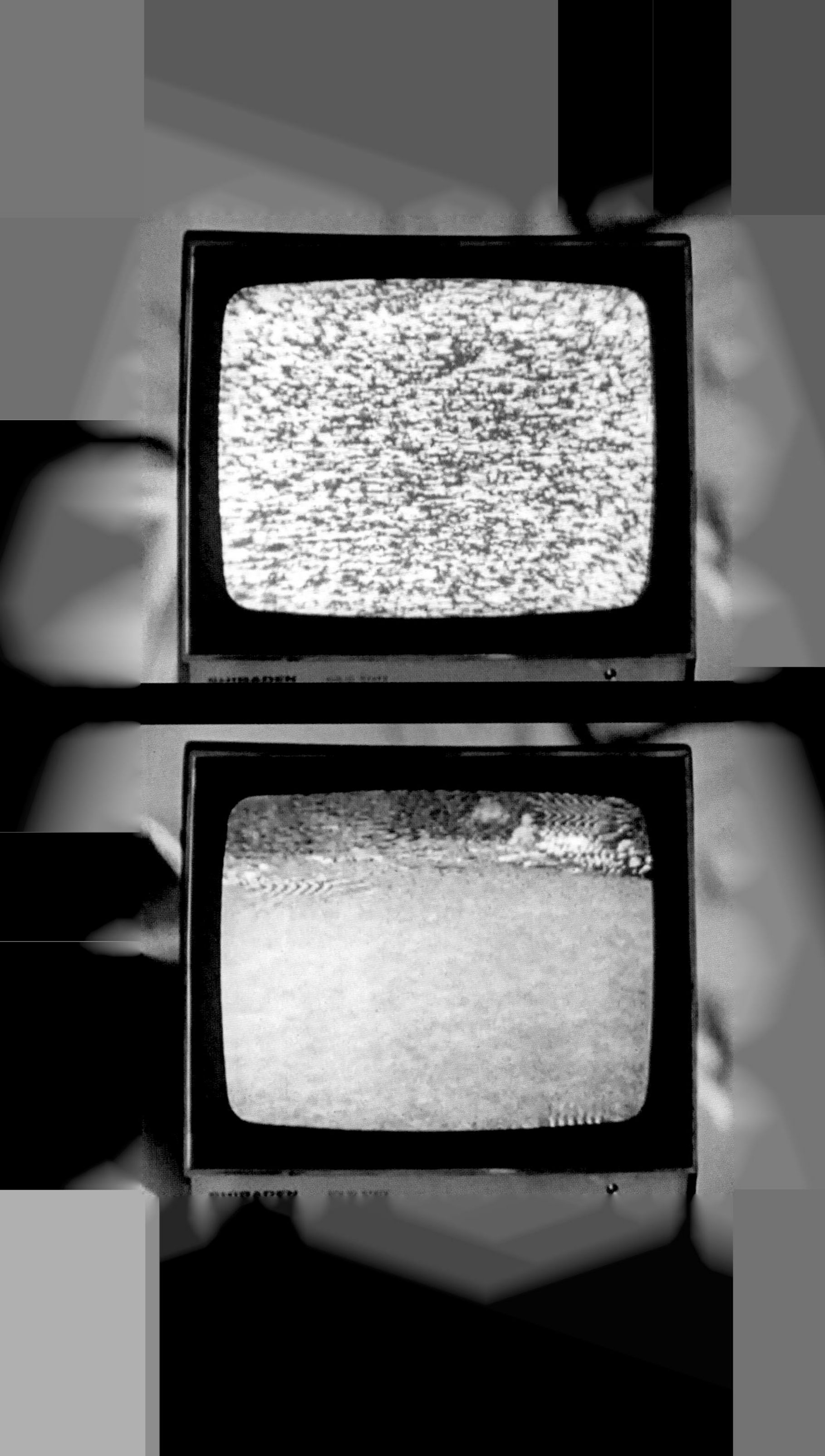

is run over, turned to a pulp, he doesn't care.

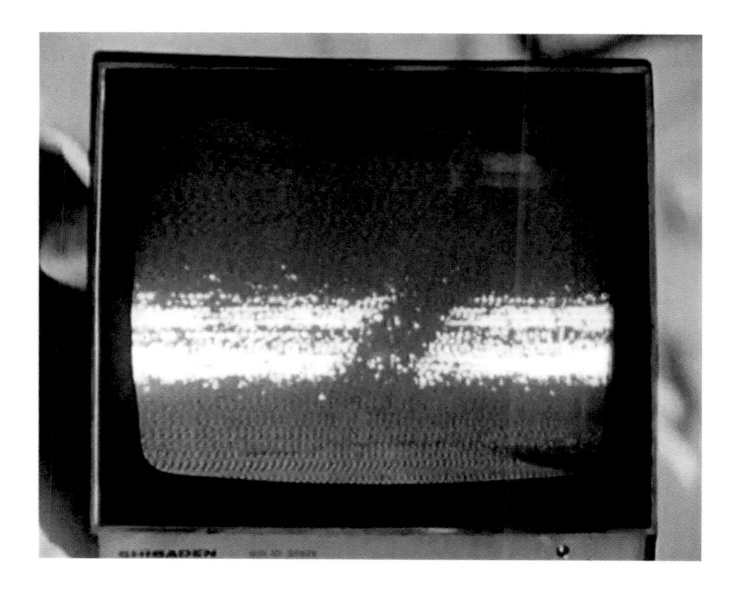

From the start there is nothing but resistance; probably always has been.

Resistance, what is resistance? Resistance is material.

The brain needs resistance.

By accumulation, does resistance have material?

Resistances.

Resistance when you look out a window; resistance when you have to write a letter—you want none of it, you *receive* a letter, again a resistance. You throw it right out; nevertheless at some point you answer.

You go out on the street, you do some shopping, you drink a beer, everything is irritating; it's all resistance.

You fall ill, you are hospitalized, things look bad — again, resistance.

Terminal illnesses suddenly appear, disappear again, they cleave to you — resistance of course.

You read books — resistance.

You want no books, you want no thoughts, you want neither language nor words, no sentences; you want no stories — you want nothing at all. Even so you fall asleep, you wake up. The consequence of falling asleep is waking up; the consequence of waking up is getting up.

You *must* get up despite all resistance.

You *must* leave the room, the paper materializes, sentences emerge, in fact always the same sentences...

from where you don't know…

Consistency, right?

Out of which resistance emerges anew again, if you are paying attention.

You want actually nothing but to doze off, forget it all.

Then suddenly the urge again…

Why darkness?

Why always the same total darkness in my books?

In short: in my books everything is *artificial* — which means all figures, events, incidents play out on a stage, and the *stage* is totally dark…

Figures appearing within a *stage* area, on a *stage* platform, are more clearly recognizable by their contours than if they appear in *natural* light, as in the usual, familiar prose.

In darkness everything becomes clear.

And this is true not only of appearances,

of the pictorial — but *also* of language. You must imagine the pages in the books...

as *completely dark*: the word flashes up,

Existenz

thereby becoming *distinct*

Existenz

or even *hyper-distinct*.

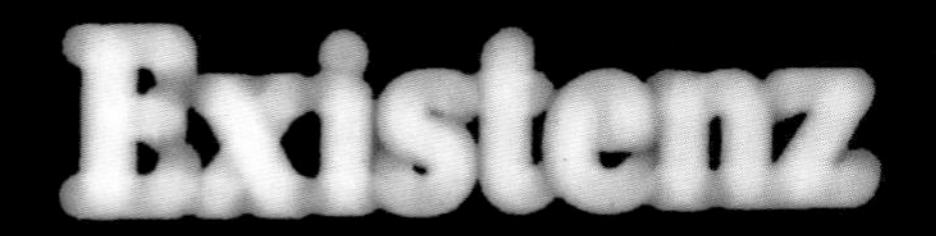

It is an artistic *device* I have used from the beginning. And when you open my work, here's what: you should imagine yourself *in the theater*; with the first page you raise *a curtain*...

the title appears,

DAS KALKWERK

total darkness — slowly from the background, out of the darkness, words, which gradually transform into *processes of external and internal nature*, made clear precisely because of their artificiality.

die einer nur im Kopf,
aber nicht auf dem Papier habe,
existiere ja gar nicht,
soll Konrad zum Baurat gesagt haben,
sagt Wieser.
Sie aufschreiben,
sie einfach aufschreiben,
denke er immer,
dieser Gedanke sei es,
die Studie einfach aufschreiben,
hinsetzen und die Studie aufschreiben,

in his head,
but not on paper,
has no real existence after all,
Konrad said to the works inspector,
according to Wieser.
I must write it down
simply write it down,
he kept thinking,
that's all there is to it,
to get it written down,
sit down and write it,

n und die S
e Existenz v
hr der Ged
Gedanke,
ie aufschrei
m Augenbl

ıdie aufsch
ll ausfülle,
ıke an die

en,
k auf den a

Th. Bernhard
R 12
12/ZW

I don't know what people understand a writer to be, but every idea regarding this is certainly wrong...

As far as I am concerned, I am no writer, I am somebody who writes...

At the same time, letters arrive from Germany, from wherever, from provincial towns, from cities, or from broadcasters or certain event organizers...

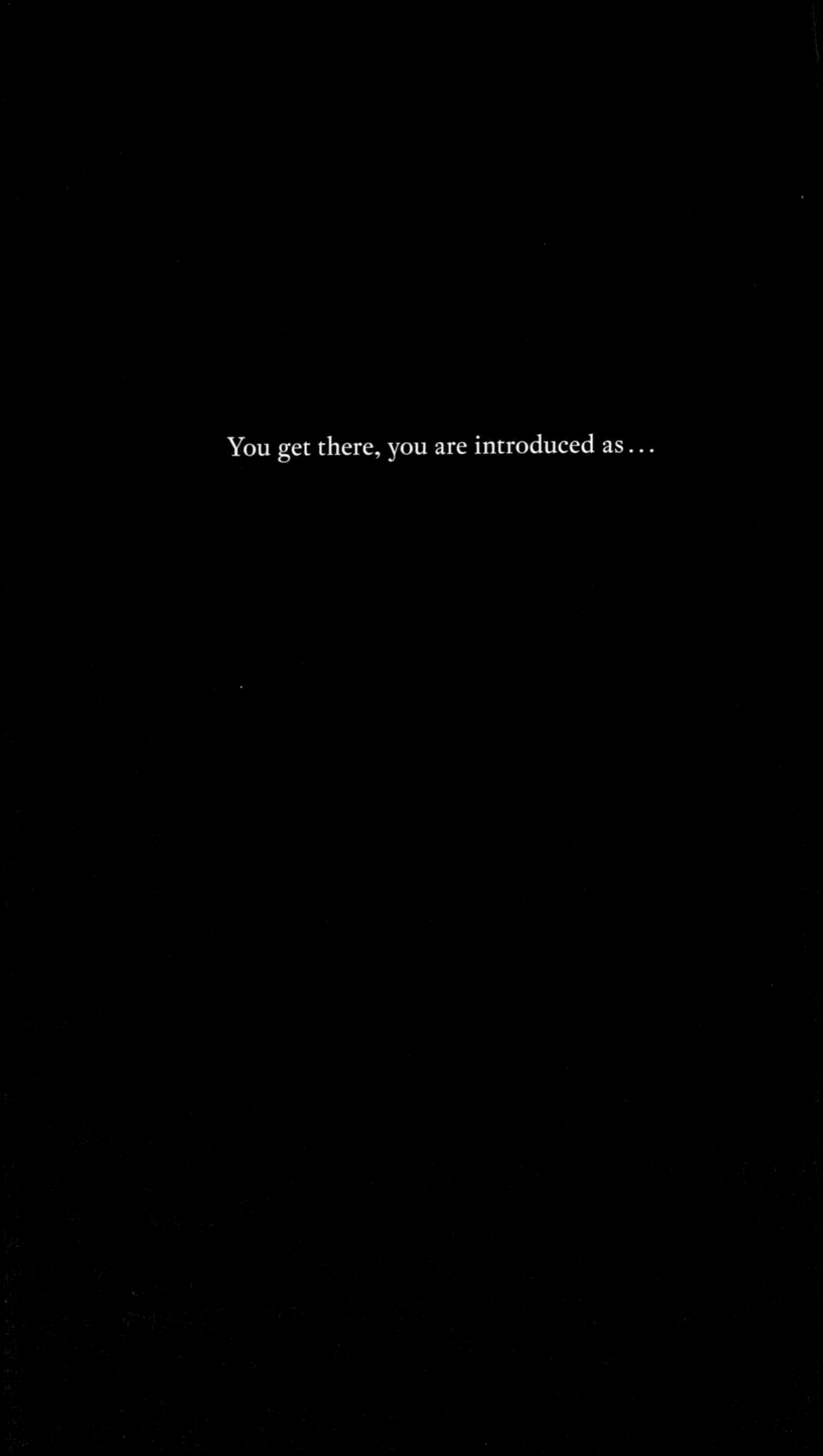
You get there, you are introduced as...

a tragic, gloomy poet, and on it goes so that you are introduced that way too in laudatory speeches, and in pseudo-scholarly papers.

Which is to say, this is an author, a writer who is to be classified in such and such a way, and the books are gloomy, the characters are gloomy, and the landscape is gloomy, and so that means — *the man* now seated before us *too is gloomy* . . .

During such a speech, in fact all that is left is some kind of gloomy . . .

lump in a dark suit...

Well, I am considered a so-called *serious* writer, the way Béla Bartók is a serious composer, and this reputation spreads...

This is essentially a very bad reputation...

I am absolutely *discomforted* by it.

Then again, of course I am hardly a cheery author, no storyteller; I basically detest stories.

I am a *story destroyer, I am the typical story destroyer.*

In my work, at the first sign of a story taking form, or if I catch sight of even a trace of a story, rising somewhere in the distance behind a mound of prose, I shoot it down.

The same is true of sentences — I almost want to annihilate in advance whole sentences that even *possibly* could develop.

On the other hand...

16/1

[What? Absolutely nothing comes to mind...]

I prefer being alone.

Essentially it is an ideal condition.

My house is also actually a vast prison.

Which I like very much — the walls the barest possible. It is bare *and* brisk. This has a very good effect on my work. The books, whatever I write, *are as is* the place I live.

Sometimes I find that the individual chapters in a book are like different rooms in this house.

The walls are alive — right? So — the pages are like walls, and that's all you need. You just have to *examine* them intently.

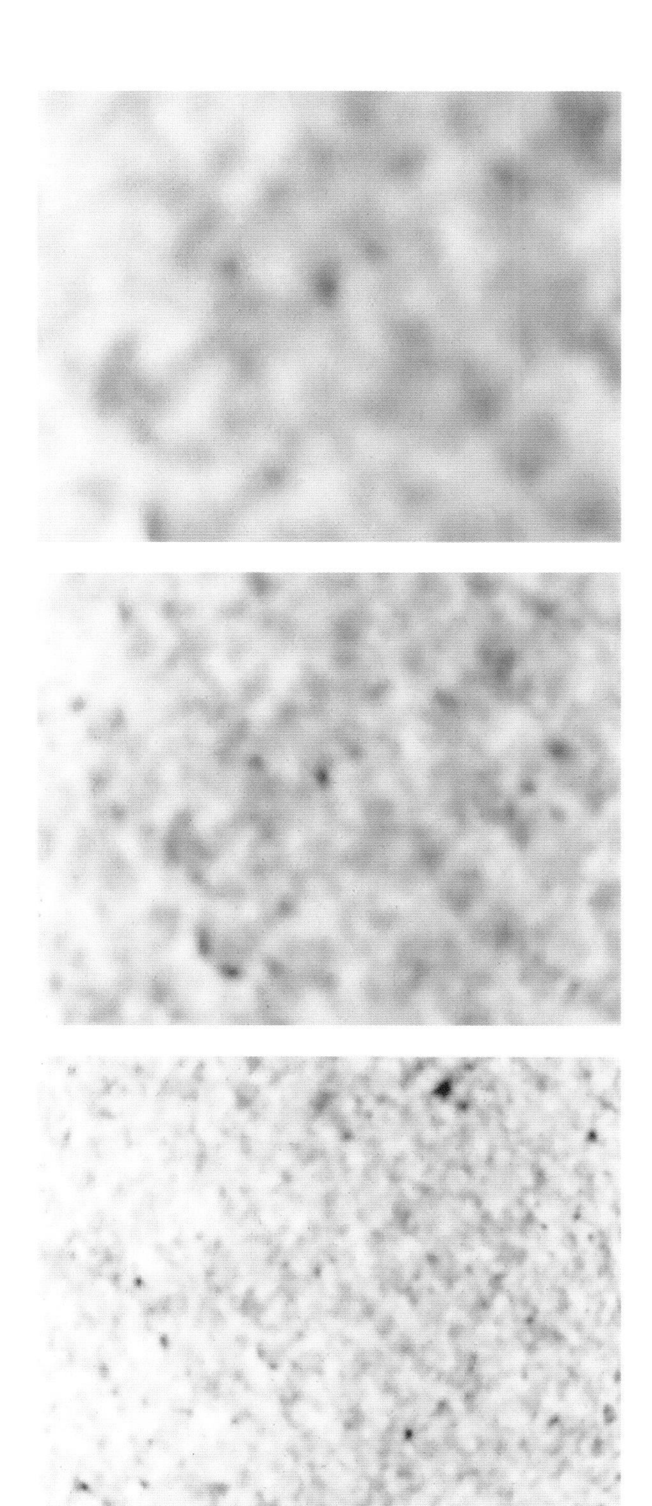

If you *scrutinize* a white wall, you realize it isn't white at all, it *isn't bare*.

If you are a long time alone, if you have accustomed yourself to solitude, are *schooled* in solitude, you discover more and more everywhere, where for the normal person there is *nothing*.

In the wall you discover cracks, little chinks, bumps, bugs. There is *tremendous* activity on the walls.

Really, the wall and the book page are perfectly alike.

To outsiders my way of life is monotonous.

All those around me live a much more exciting, or if
not exactly exciting, at least interesting life...

To me the lives of my neighbors, who *pursue*
quite simple trades — my neighbor is a farmer, a
papermaker lives across the way, next door to him
is a carpenter, farther away are only papermakers,
craftsmen, farmers — which I find interesting... an
occupation that, it seems to me, although done a
hundred thousand times the same way, and *continues*,
is continually new.

My own life, my own occupation, my own day to me
seems monotonous, flat, meaningless...

STUDIO HBG.
1

Most horrible of all for me is writing prose...

The very most difficult...

And from the moment I realized and knew that,
I have sworn to write only prose.

I could have done something completely different.
I learned a good number of other disciplines, but
none horrible.

For instance, when I was very young I took drawing
lessons, and I probably could have become a passable
illustrator; it came to me very easily.

I studied music, and it came very easily to me to play instruments, to create music — to compose, that is.

For a while I thought I'd definitely become a conductor.

I studied the aesthetics of music and one instrument after another, and because it came to me only *too easily*...

I gave it all up.

Then I could have become an actor or director or dramaturge. There was a time when that had me very captivated. It was very exciting; I acted a lot, most of all in comical roles, and directed...

I also went to a business school and there was even a time when I thought, sure, I could be a businessman, too, and it was tempting to go in that direction...

And very early —

up until age seventeen, eighteen — I hated nothing so much as books…

I lived with my grandfather, who wrote and had an immense library, and being together with these books all the time, having to pass through this library, every day, was just horrible for me…

And probably…

Why in fact did I come to write, why do I write books?

Out of opposition to myself, suddenly, and against this condition — because to me, as I've said, resistance is *everything*...

I wanted exactly this tremendous resistance, and that's why I write prose...

It may have been because of being put in the hospital for a year when I was eighteen; I lay there and received — I think it's still called this today — the *Extreme Unction*.

Then I was put in a sanatorium — and I lay there high in the mountains, months on end.

It was *always the same mountain* before me.

There was a plank bed with a gray blanket, and I lay there under a woolen cover through autumn and winter, day and night, in the open air.

Out of sheer boredom — because you can't just incessantly lie in front of *one* mountain without doing anything — I mean, I couldn't even move — I began to write. That was probably *the why and wherefore*.

And out of this boredom and in isolation with this mountain, the one called *Heukareck* that rises over Schwarzach St. Veit some 6,900 feet... looking at it month after month, always the same — because it lies on the shady side, it never changes — either you'll go mad or begin to write...

So I took up pencil and paper there, made myself notes, and by writing overcame the hatred of books and of writing and of pencil and pen, and this surely is the root of the evils I now have to contend with...

Primarily I want nothing but to be left alone.

This is very demanding, and over time external events, too, no longer interest me.

They are, after all, always the same.

That's for others to deal with.

Only my own affairs interest me, and I can be very ruthless.

And whether I am at my country home or in one city or another — Brussels, or Vienna, or Salzburg, wherever, it's all the same — if everything around me should collapse or turn even more ridiculous than it already is, or not...

It has absolutely no meaning to me, and it doesn't do a thing for me, least of all enlighten me...

And so...

[Well, enough...]

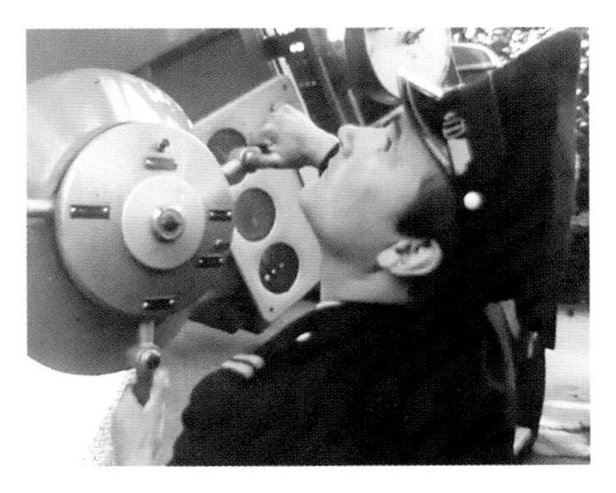

ALEMANIA 2
BULGARIA 1

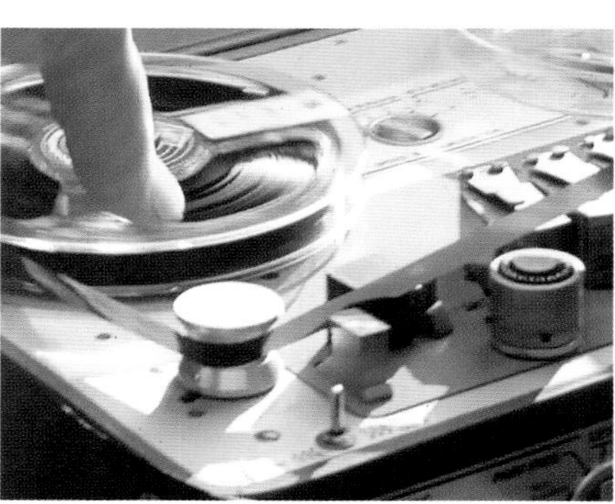

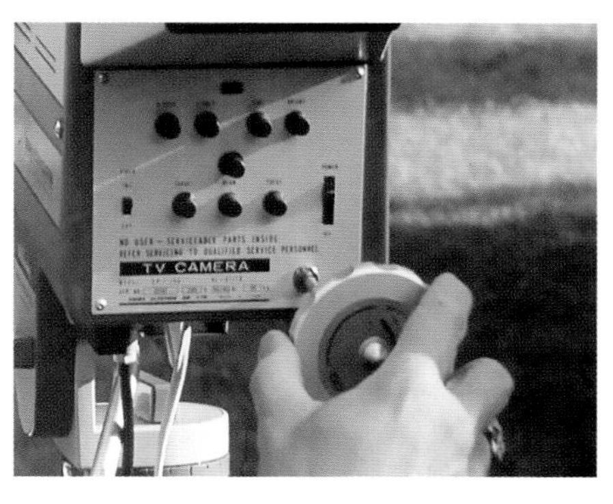
NO USER— SERVICEABLE PARTS INSIDE
REFER SERVICING TO QUALIFIED SERVICE PERSONNEL
TV CAMERA

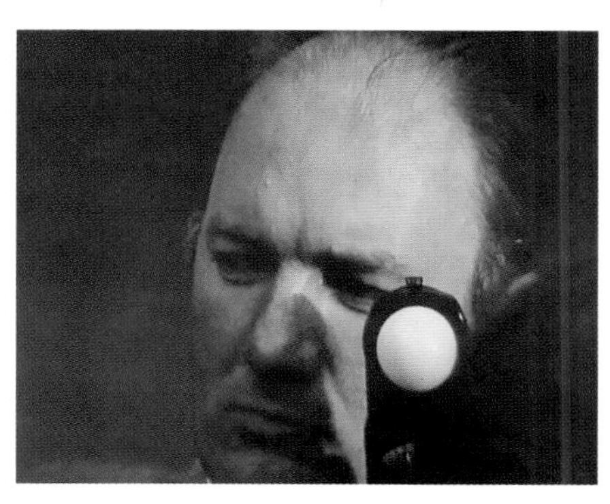

THIRD DAY

3. TAG

Bernhard
R23

Yes, interaction with philosophy, written text is
the most treacherous... for me in particular...

I often churn the mess over for hours, days,
weeks long...

I want no contact; I want none of it.

Then again, it's also so that the very authors who are the most important for me are my toughest opponents, or enemies.

It is an incessant fight against the very same to whom you are *totally* addicted.

And I am addicted to Musil, Pavese, Ezra Pound—it's really not poetry; it is *absolute prose.*

In very simple sentences a landscape is built; in a few words in Pavese's diary, a passage by Lermontov, of course Dostoyevsky, Turgenev, basically all Russians...

Apart from Valéry the French never interested me at all... Valéry's *Monsieur Teste* — is a book so thoroughly thumbed, I have to buy it again and again; it is always pored over, frayed, in tatters...

Henry James — a constant fight. It is a bitter enmity... always reeling...

Mostly you feel ridiculous up against these people, which means you mustn't work...

But little by little you gain command, over even the very great... and you can subdue them...

You can rise above Virginia Woolf or Forster, and *then I have to write.*

And comparison is exactly the art you must try to master.

It is the only school that has any point and that will take you farther and forward.

There can be nothing whole; you've got to smash it to pieces.

The successful, the beautiful becomes ever more suspicious.

At the most unanticipated point possible you've got to abandon...

So it is wrong, too…

to write a *so-called chapter* in a book really to the end. It is, just so, wrong to write any book to the end. And *the biggest mistake* is when an author writes a book to the end.

In one's contact with others, too, it is very good to *suddenly break off* a relationship.

Melancholia is a very pleasant condition. I succumb to it very easily and gladly. Less often, or not at all, in the country, where I work, but in the city, instantly...

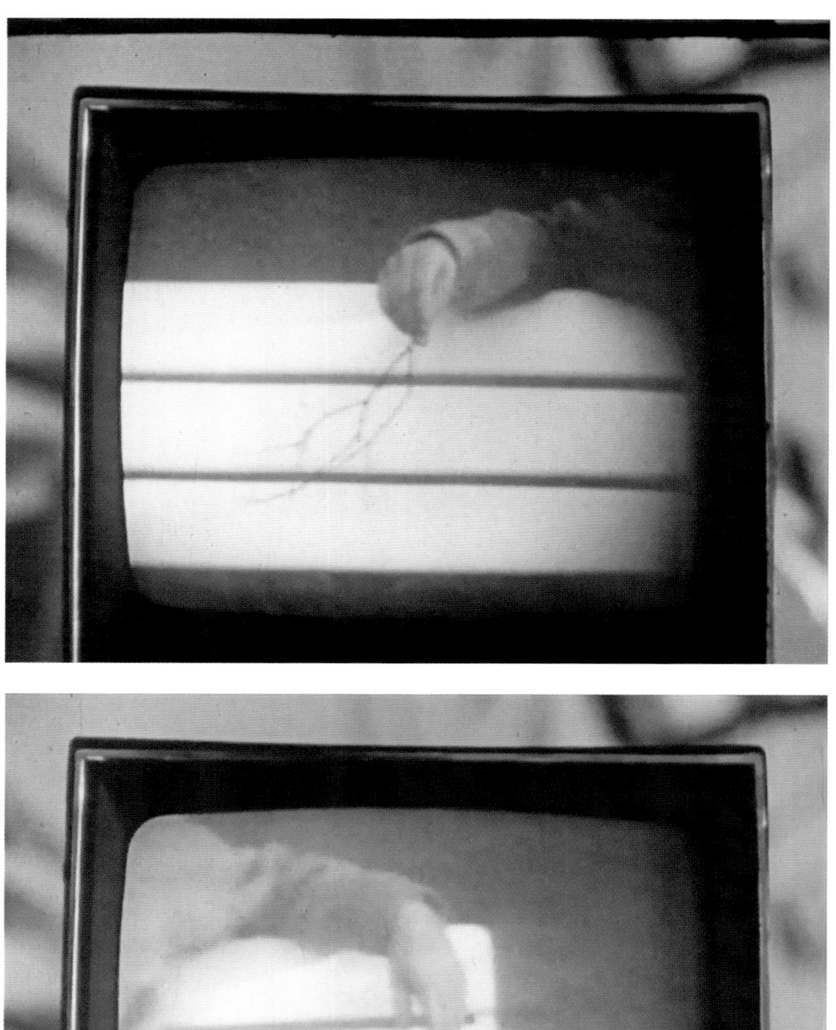

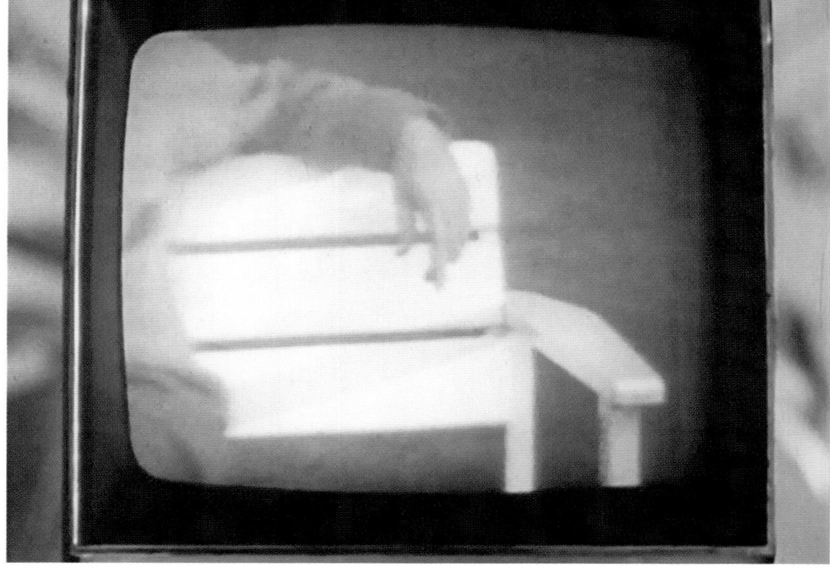

To me, there is no place lovelier than Vienna and the melancholia I have and always have had in the city…

It's the people there I have known for two decades who are melancholia…

It's the streets of Vienna. It is the atmosphere of this city, of *the city of studying, naturally.*

It's sentences, always the same, that people there say to me, probably the same that *I* say to these people, a wonderful precondition for melancholia.

You sit in a park somewhere, hours long; in a café, hours long — melancholia.

It's the young writers of the past, young no more.

Suddenly you notice, this is no longer a young man anymore; he *acts like* a young man — probably *like I* act like a young man but am *a young man no more.*

And this compounds over time but becomes quite nice.

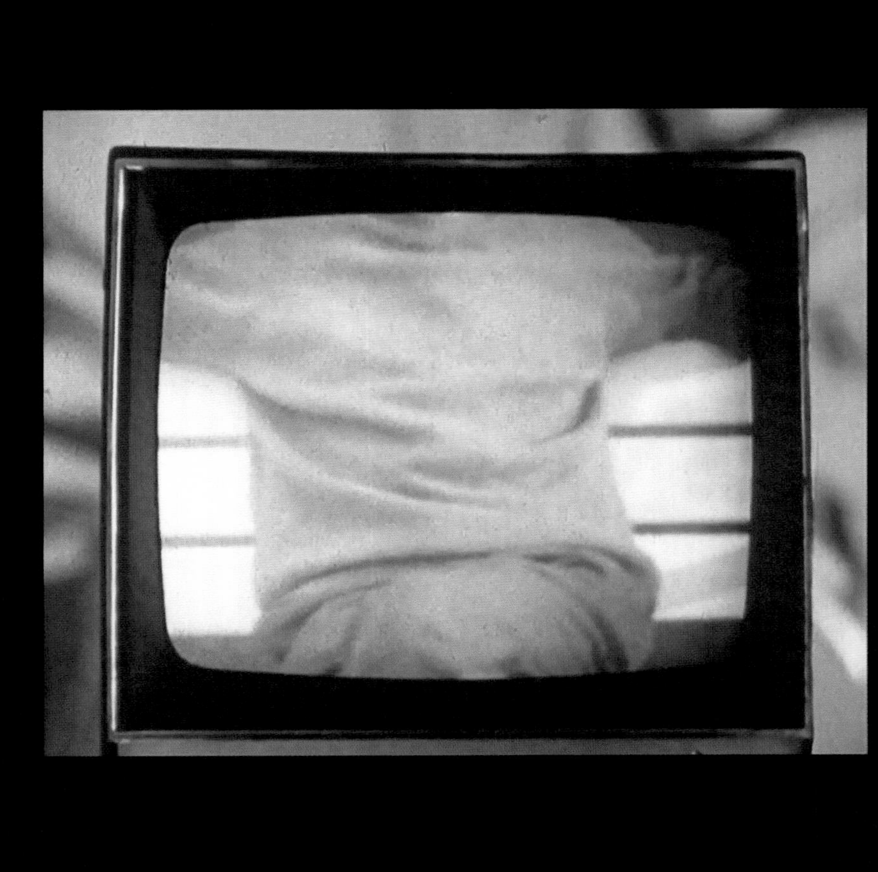

I very much enjoy going to the cemeteries in Vienna, to the Döblinger cemetery right nearby me, or the cemetery in Neustift am Walde, and I look forward to the epitaphs, the names I know from days gone by.

Melancholia, when you enter a shop: the same sales clerk who moved *so incredibly quickly* twenty years ago *is now very slow.*

She pours the sugar *slowly* into the sack. It is a completely other movement now by which she takes the money, closes the cash register drawer...

It's the same ring of the bell at the door, but it is melancholia.

And this condition may persist for weeks.

And I think, maybe melancholia is the ideal or the only useful remedy; the continued taking of melancholia in pill form for me...

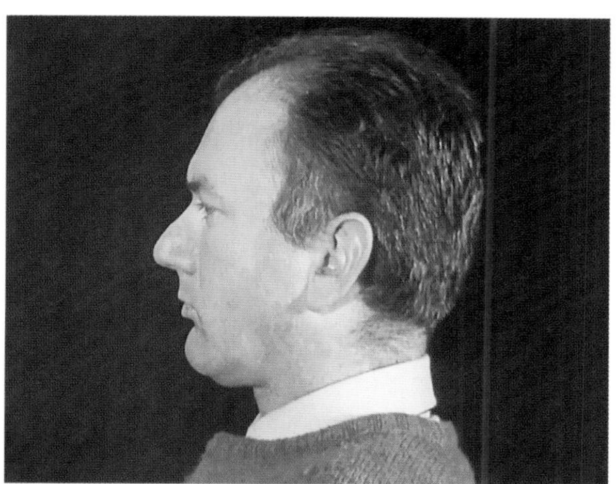

It is always the conversation with my brother that does not exist, the conversation with my mother that does not exist.

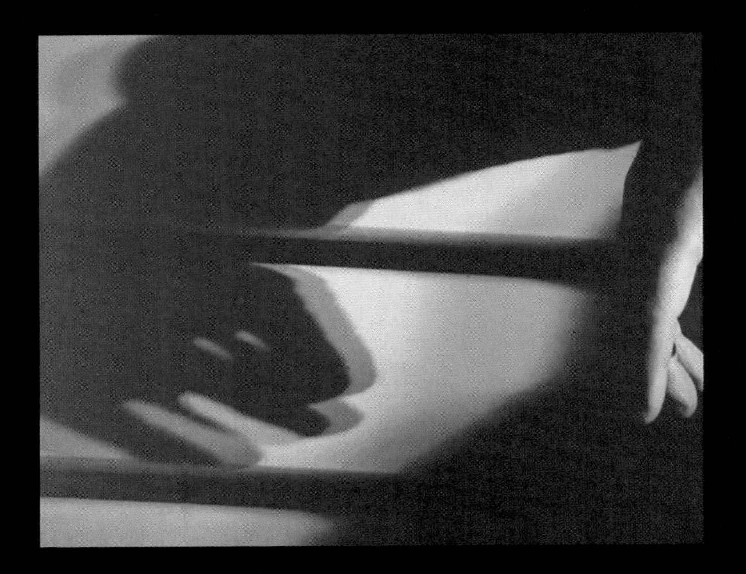

It is the conversation with the father that also does not exist. It is the conversation with the past that does not exist, and *which* no longer exists, *which will never exist.*

It is the conversation with great sentences that do not exist. It is the talk with *nature* that does not exist, the engagement with the concepts that are no concepts, *can be no concepts.*

The engagement with conceptlessness, weak-mindedness.

It is the engagement with a material that is unrelentingly incomplete.

The conversation with a matter that does not answer.

It is the *absolute* silence...

that ruins everything, the *absolute* despair from which you can no longer escape.

It is the imaginary opposition you have created only to be able to keep *imagining* it.

It is the attempt just to touch…

objects that disintegrate the very instant you think you have touched them.

It is the engagement with facts that prove to be errors.

It is the attempt to bridge a time *that never existed.*

It is always the same imagination toward an idea that by nature can turn out only false.

It is the identification with things grown out of sentences, and of these things, you know nothing; nor of the sentences; and, as ever, you know nothing at all.

This is *daily life, from which you* must distance yourself. You have got to *leave it all*, not *close* the door behind you but *slam it shut* and *walk away*.

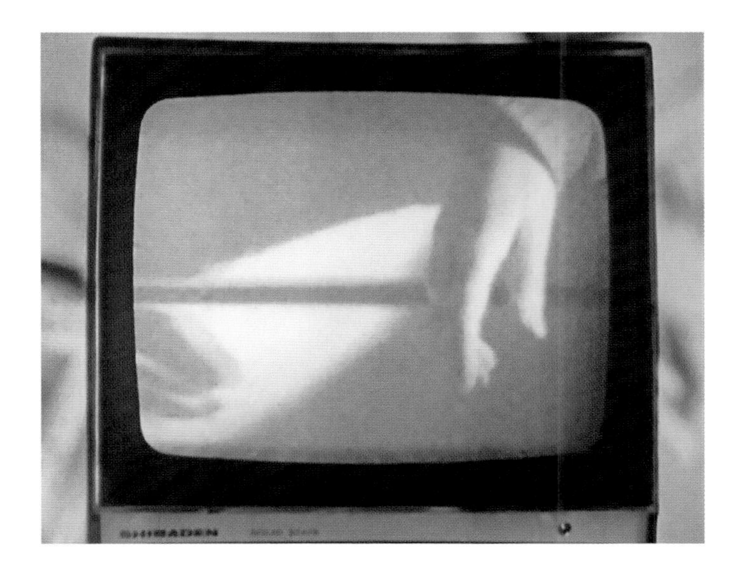

And everything must of its own accord recede and, without a sound, *disappear.*

From the *one* darkness, impossible to master in an entire lifetime, now become finally totally impossible, you have to enter the *other*, *the second*, *the ultimate* darkness before you and get through as quickly as possible, with no hesitation, no philosophical hairsplitting, just go in . . . and, if possible, by closing your eyes *precede* the darkness and open your eyes again only when you have certainty that you absolutely are in the darkness, in the ultimate one.

Notes

In the summer of 1970, days and days into a search that became personally utterly preposterous to find a suitable locale, I settled once and for all on a white-painted bench in a park in a suburb of Hamburg, in order, as agreed, to say before the director Ferry Radax some sentences about myself, to make statements that occurred to me coincidentally and haphazardly as I said and made them, in fact in a state of extreme irritation, as is more or less inherent to the nature of such an undertaking; they seem to me today as well, having seen the film and heard the statements made by me in the film, more or less coincidental and haphazard. I said much on the bench (and thus in the film) just *so* and not elsewise, although I could have said it completely another way than as it is published here with the title *Three Days*. The fact, however, that a film was being made in which my person should sit on a white-painted bench in a suburban Hamburg park for fifty-five minutes solid with no purpose the whole time other than to say (or not to say) whatever came to mind, with no concern (and therefore must needs be concerned) *why* I said what I said and not *how* I said what I said, and the fact the film that resulted was in the end to be accepted led directly to the idea for the astonishing director with his astonishing work methods (as I observed during the three days in Hamburg) to write a longer, i.e., minimum hour-and-a-half-long film, in accordance with this method of working. *That* and the pleasure of making such a *work as an experiment* was the distinct occasion to write, from the early fragment *The Italian* — now suddenly suitable, but which in fact lay unfinished, and which I had already forgotten about — an *approximately precise production*, actually largely divergent from the fragment though essentially in every respect relating back to the fragment as I had intended it, for the film that Radax, over several successive winter weeks of 1971, made without me.

Th. B.

Thomas Bernhard: Drei Tage was first published together with *Der Italiener* in 1989.

Afterword
Resistance and Productive Inefficiency

On Ferry Radax's Television Portrait *Thomas Bernhard: Three Days*

Georg Vogt

PREHISTORY

By 1970, when Ferry Radax began work on his film *Thomas Bernhard: Drei Tage*, among the few constants known in his diverse cinematic work were his films involving literature. Alongside literary adaptations and numerous writers' portraits, what stood out most prominently were Radax's frequent collaborations with authors. Characteristic of such work is his best-known film, *Sonne halt!* [Sun stop!, 1960], shot in Italy and made with Konrad Bayer, a member of the circle of artists known as the Wiener Gruppe.

After promising beginnings in the 1950s, employment as an independent filmmaker in Austria grew increasingly difficult, and after some hiatuses in the 1960s, Radax gravitated to German television. When Wolfgang Kudrnovsky established the series *Nachtstudio* on ORF [Austrian Broadcasting Corporation], it gave Radax a place where he could create artists' portraits free of creative constraints. In 1967 he completed the portrait collection *Forum Dichter Graz* [Graz Writers' Forum] and a feature on the author, poet, and leader among Austria's avant-garde H. C. Artmann. Radax also shot numerous films over the next several years for WDR [German Broadcasting Corporation], including his documentary/fiction portrait *Konrad Bayer, oder: die welt bin ich und das ist meine sache* [Konrad Bayer, or: i am the world and that's my business] about his friend Konrad Bayer, who meanwhile had committed suicide at the age of thirty-two.

With the success of the Bayer film, which won the 1970 Rudolf Grimme Prize for best experimental work, Radax had established himself and hoped for further literary-cinematic collaborations. He sought out Thomas Bernhard to make a film of Bernhard's novel *Verstörung* [*Gargoyles*]. Although neither the author nor the television station showed interest (and a film version of *Verstörung* has yet to be realized), Radax was nonetheless commissioned to produce a portrait of Bernhard.

Radax envisioned creating the portrait in nine sequences, each anticipated to take a day of shooting, and he drafted a specific, hermetic concept for the staging: Bernhard's role would be to illustrate Radax's interpretation of him and of his work.

Filming was planned for June 1970 in Hamburg, where Bernhard was staying during rehearsals of his play *Ein Fest für Boris* [*A Party for Boris*]. Radax took the opportunity to complete work on another Bayer piece: *Der Kopf des Vitus Bering* [The head of Vitus Bering], shot on a single day immediately before the start of work on *Drei Tage*. Radax invited Bernhard to the filming to give him an impression of his film work.

RESISTANCE

Shortly before the start of filming, Bernhard objected that Radax's formal concepts did not mesh with the author's often-espoused poetics of story destruction. Now, at the eleventh hour, the resistance described in the film took real form. Bernhard watched the shooting of *Vitus Bering* as planned but withdrew his cooperation on the morning of the first day of filming his own portrait.

He was skeptical of Radax's complex staging concept—he did not want to become the actor of his own person as conceived by someone else. A compromise was reached to avoid canceling the project altogether. Bernhard would sit on a bench and say what was going through his mind. The flow of associations would be initiated by a series of key words and phrases that Radax had compiled in a notebook. Bernhard was thus simply to interact with his own text fragments and with the cinematic apparatus, which Radax had to adapt on the fly to the new circumstances.

Rather than the planned nine days, three would have to suffice. In addition to the 16mm camera on hand, a video system was procured to allow uninterrupted filming, more perspectives for the montage, and greater freedom in camera work. Video technology enabled Bernhard to watch what he had already said and return to it afterward. The only framework now would be that over the course of the three days the camera would make a continual approach toward the author, and the montage would follow the sequence of the monologue. From a starting distance of 500 feet, by the end of filming the cameras closed in to a mere 20 inches. On each individual day, filming was done first in the morning, and then afternoon, and on the third day in the evening as well. The resulting continuity of time and place is the only hint — at most, merely an ironic comment — of the strict form that had been abandoned in a film that distinctly rejects the conventional.

The original plan had given way to an experiment that would unfold in the performative moment through the interaction of participants and the location. As with the earlier *Sonne halt!* and *Mosaik im Vertrauen*, such wide-open parameters allowed for improvisation and for a film that developed through situational reaction — what Radax calls "what the film itself calls for."

An aesthetic of productive inefficiency came to dominate the finished film. Bernhard sits, the camera rolls, and often actually nothing is happening. Chance occasionally intervenes, creating fragments that in editing find various places in the film. A bird hopping by in the foreground counterpoints Bernhard's silence; the roar of an airplane amplifies his expression.

Time and surplus film footage meant not only the possibility of suspending conventional television and film industry rules, but the very possibility of putting together a portrait suitable for Bernhard.

The black transitions Radax used as a connecting device in the montage signal his omissions and cuts but function thematically as well. For the most part, Bernhard's voice dominates the soundtrack. The camera observes him, tracks his gestures and rhythms, his swinging foot, a swaying branch.

Yet the gaze of the camera is by no means limited to Bernhard. It strolls across the entire set and sometimes seems to want to free itself entirely from the component of sound. While the camera can vary the playing field of sound, throughout the film it remains inextricable from live sound; a complete emancipation is denied. The camera may only alter distance and explore movements. At times Bernhard is pushed to the edge of the frame, cut off, or simply replaced, by an empty bench, a nearby tree, or the activity of making the film itself. Associative spaces emerge and oscillate between elucidation, confusion, refusal, and reflection on the conditions of production.

SELF-REFLECTION

Self-reflective moments fill the first two days; production conditions are demonstrated, creating a distance from the present moment. On the third day exposition completely overtakes the film's progress, creating a distance from the film itself for ten minutes.

With a nod to the aesthetics of kabuki theater, at the start of the third day the focal point shifts from Bernhard to preparatory tasks for the final day of filming. A tall film crane is raised—which will be used for just a single take, an aerial view from high above of all busying themselves in preparation for the last act. The activities shown have to do only with the filming itself; they do not relate to Bernhard. As the third day begins, the distance to the author that has been achieved is reversed by extreme nearness.

Bernhard, now filmed in tight close-up, is shown in white balance and focus tests, frontally and in profile, as though posing for mugshots after an arrest. Toward the end of the film the point of view becomes so magnified as to transform into abstraction.

We seem to have grown close; Bernhard speaks of ways out and ultimate causes. The materiality of his clothing fills the screen of the video camera, while a second take in which he is headless pushes him toward the edge of Christian iconography. Here, too, on the verge of an unobstructed nearness to the author Radax withdraws; by filming the image displayed on the video camera's monitor he points to the artificiality of the situation. Framing and alienation create a distance from which the fascination of Bernhard the author and his aesthetic may be experienced.

BERNHARD'S REACTION

Radax edited the film, without Bernhard's involvement, to fit the required television format of fifty-four minutes. Radax cut large portions as well as little details in Bernhard's spoken text in his montage. Having taken many liberties with these omissions, Radax faced the prescreening with Bernhard rather nervously. On many occasions and in interviews Radax has recalled watching from an adjacent room from which he could catch only a glimpse of what he had already noticed as a major mood indicator during filming: the rhythmic swing of Bernhard's foot as he sat on the bench and spoke on camera. Although Radax took the same movement as an initial positive indication, he was well aware that Bernhard was known to argue over the smallest details in the print versions of his texts. He was pleasantly surprised that Bernhard approved of the film without any alterations. Radax recalls Bernhard commenting, "The film made me incredibly anxious; every time I thought here comes something that I should not have said, you had, thank god, cut it."

Bernhard was also very eager to continue the collaboration, as he was fascinated with the artistic methods Radax used in *Three Days*. He granted him the rights for a filmic adaptation of *Verstörung*, a film that was never made. Bernhard also adapted his own short text *Der Italiener* as the basis for a second collaboration that ocurred in 1972. The transcript of *Three Days* was later published in German with *Der Italiener* and became one of the most frequently cited autobiographical sources about Bernhard.

GEORG VOGT is a lecturer at the Institute for Theater, Film, and Media Studies at the University of Vienna. He is co-editor, with Otto Mörth and Isabella Hirt, of the German monograph on Radax, *Vision, Utopie, Experiment: Ferry Radax* (Vienna: Sonderzahl, 2014). He completed his thesis in 2007 on the film *Thomas Bernhard: Drei Tage*, and collaborated on the publication of the film on DVD with Index (Index No. 035; see www.index-dvd.at).

Ferry Radax © Croci & du Fresne Fotografie

FERRY RADAX (b. 1932) lives in Hollenburg, Austria. He has worked as an author, cameraman, editor, director, and also as a producer of documentaries, experimental works, advertisements, fiction, series, music, and dramatic works in many places worldwide.

SELECTED FILMS BY FERRY RADAX

Das Floß [The raft], 1954, experimental film

Mosaik im Vertrauen [Mosaic sub rosa], 1955, experimental film with Peter Kubelka

Sonne halt! [Sun stop!], 1959–62, experimental film

Hundertwasser, 1965, artist's portrait

H. C. Artmann, 1967, experimental writer's portrait

Konrad Bayer, oder: die welt bin ich und das ist meine sache [Konrad Bayer, or: i am the world and that's my business], 1969, experimental docudrama

Thomas Bernhard: Drei Tage [Thomas Bernhard: Three Days], 1970, writer's portrait

Der Kopf des Vitus Bering [The head of Vitus Bering], 1970, explorer's portrait, after a work by Konrad Bayer

Der Italiener [The Italian], 1971–72, drama, after Thomas Bernhard's story

Ludwig Wittgenstein, 1973–76, philosopher's portrait

Wer sind Sie, Mr. Joyce? [Who are you, Mr. Joyce?], 1980, writer's portrait

Hundertwasser—Leben in Spiralen [Hundertwasser—Life in spirals], 1996–98, second artist's portrait

SELECTED AWARDS

Internationaler Experimentalfilmpreis [International experimental film prize]
Mosaik im Vertrauen, France, 1956

Österreichischer Filmförderungspreis [Austrian film advancement prize]
Hundertwasser, Austria, 1967

Adolf Grimme Fernsehpreis [Adolf Grimme television prize]
Konrad Bayer, oder: die welt bin ich und das ist meine sache, Germany, 1970

Adolf Grimme Spezialpreis (x3) [Adolf Grimme special prize]
Der Italiener, Germany, 1972

Österreichisches Ehrenkreuz für Wissenschaft und Kunst, 1. Klasse [Austrian honor cross for science and art, first class, lifetime achievement]
Lebenswerk, Austria, 2003

Ehrenmedaille der Bundeshauptstadt Wien in Gold [Municipal gold medal of Vienna award, lifetime achievement]
Lebenswerk, Austria, 2008

Niederösterreichischer Kulturpreis Würdigungspreis Medienkunst, Austria, 2012 [Lower Austrian culture prize for media art]

For a complete filmography visit www.ferryradax.at

Appendix

The following selection of pages with quotes and fragments from Bernhard's *Frost* are from a notebook Ferry Radax prepared for the production of *Drei Tage*. Bernhard kept the notebook alongside him while seated on the bench and referred to it to spark his thoughts.

WORDS

Fr 8 ...whom one can *by all means* call cretinous

Fr 9 The walker type...a misanthrope

Fr 9 Books: Koltz, diseases of the brain, Henry James
Quote

Fr 10 In the sudden PALPABLE quiet...
Quote

Fr 11 a millenium before civilized life...
Quote

Fr 21 to confront with formidable strength

Fr 57 master contemner of reality...malefaction machinist...denier of human will

Fr 58 The words "never"..."school"..."death"..."burial" had stalked and irritated him for years.

Fr 60 emissaries of defeat (and childhood memories)

Fr 62 haughtiness, abandonment, severity, deadly solitude.

Fr 66 I work with my own concepts. Knowledge detracts from knowledge, you know?

Fr 67 bearers of opinions with different speed limits.

Fr 91 With a unnatural speed for his age.

Fr 104 Then they detonated again...and the air pressure slapped against the cliff walls.

Wo — 1 —

Fr 8 Wo ... die man <u>Ruhig</u> schwachsinnig nennen kann

Fr 9 Wo Spaziergängertypus ... Menschenhasser

Fr 9 Wo Bücher: Koltz, Gehirnkrankheiten, Henry James
<u>Zitat</u>

Fr 1o Wo In der plötzlichen GROBEN Ruhe ...
<u>Zitat</u>

Fr 11 Wo Vormenschenwürdiges Jahrtausend.
<u>Zitat</u>

Fr 21 Wo Mit ungeheurer Kraft ... vorzugehen.

Fr 57 Wo Wirklichkeitsverachtungsmagister ... Gesetzesverbrecherma-
schinist ... Menschenwillenverschweiger

Fr 58 Wo Das Wort "Nie" ... "Schule" ... "Tod" ... "Leichenbegängnis"
haben ihn jahrelang verfolgt und irritiert.

Fr 6o Wo Niederlagenheraufbeförderer (und Kindheitserinnerungen)

Fr 62 Wo Übermut, Verlassenheit, Strenge, tödliche Einsamkeit.

Fr 66 Wo Ich arbeite mit meinen Begriffen. Wissen lenkt von Wissen
ab, wissen Sie?

Fr 67 Wo Ansichtenträger verschiedener Geschwindigkeitsbegrenzung.

Fr 91 Wo Mit unheimlicher Altersgeschwindigkeit.

Fr 1o4 Wo Dann sprengten sie wieder ... und der Luftdruck ohrfeigt die
Felswände.

COLD

Fr 19 One freezes from the inside.

Fr 22 Even the... imagination, everything.

Fr 24 In winter they freeze to death, as I said, on the way to school.

Fr 29 Because in the gorge it's surely very cold.

Fr 30 It's chilling.

Fr 33 As if everything had been frozen solid under a sheet of ice.

Fr 38 Here the painter drew him back with the word "ice-cold."

Fr 39 You could freeze to death "between two thoughts."

Fr 64 The cold has increased.

Fr 80 Outside, the world clenches up from the cold.
For hours I can't warm up from the cold.

Fr 81 And suddenly it's cold, I'm shivering... *Quote*

Fr 82 And then: "What's it like in the parsonage?
Cold?" — "Yes, he says, "very cold, really cold."
It's got to be cold, down there.

Fr 97 I ignore the cold.

JKä   - 1 -

Fr 19 Kä Man friert innerlich.

Fr 22 Kä Selbst die ... Phantasie, alles.

Fr 24 Kä Im Winter erfrieren sie, wie gesagt, auf dem Schulweg.

Fr 29 Kä Weil es im Hohlweg sicher sehr kalt ist.

Fr 3o Kä Es zieht grauenhaft.

Fr 33 Kä Wie wenn alles unter einer Eisdecke erstarrt gewesen wäre.

Fr 38 Kä Da zog ihn der Maler durch ein Wort wieder zurück, an sich, mit dem Wort "eiskalt".

Fr 39 Kä Erfrieren käme "zwischen zwei Gedanken"

Fr 64 Kä Die Kälte hat zugenommen.

Fr 8o Kä Draußen zieht sich die Welt zusammen vor Kälte. Ich kann mich stundenlang nicht erwärmen vor Kälte.

Fr 81 Kä Und es ist plötzlich kalt, mich friert... Zitat

Fr 82 Kä Und dann: Wie ist es im Pfarrhaus? Kalt? - ja, sagte er, sehr kalt, recht kalt.
Es muß doch kalt sein, da unten ...

Fr 97 Kä Ich ignoriere die Kälte.

SEX

Fr 7 The landlady disgusts me . . . child . . . slaughterhouse doorways. (Reference to dissection)

Fr 7 Silently she seemed . . . (subjunctive question [Janko] Musulin MAZ [video interview] Bernhard's answer) . . . sudden nausea (Bernhard's discomfort)

Fr 12 The roadsides invite debauchery?

Fr 13 Their beds . . . one horror to another.

Fr 14 Sexuality . . . a sex life, not a life. *Quote*

Fr 17 . . . dislike the landlady.

Fr 21 Landlady with beef.

Fr 22 (Masochism?) Such thoughts . . . immoral . . . repellent . . . great abuses, which he even sought out. *Quote* worked up to the height of insanity

Fr 25 All conceived in drunkenness.

Fr 25 . . . people only really want a pig, not a kid.

Fr 45 WAR is essentially the THIRD sex.

Fr 54 (Sex and crime) . . . She just turned away from the village square. Straight into criminality.

Fr 55 (Masochism) Otherwise, the landlady was "a creature that will take a beating, hole up a while, and then come back out as if nothing had happened."

Fr 57 Where ugliness ingratiates itself everywhere like a "sexual compulsion."

Fr 111 This artist fornication . . . paradisiacal shamelessness . . . *Quote* to nothing but insipid and boastful.

Se — 1 —

Fr 7 Se Mich ekelt vor der Wirtin ... Kind ... Schlachthaustüren.
Me (Bezug zum Sezieren)

Fr 7 Se Stillschweigend schien sie mich ... (Konjunktivfrage Musulin MAZ, Antwort Bernhard)... Plötzliche Übelkeit (Unruhe Bernhard)

Fr 12 Se Die Wegränder verführen zur Unzucht?

Fr 13 Se
Fü Ihre Betten ... Das andere Fürchterliche.

Fr 14 Se Das Geschlechtliche, ... ein Geschlechtsleben, kein Leben. Zitat

Fr 17 Se ... Wirtin mißfällt.

Fr 21 Se Ad 7 Wirtin mit Rindfleisch.

Fr 22 Se (Masochismus ?) Solche Gedanken ... unzüchtig ... abweisend ... große Mißhandlungen, die er ja suche.
Zitat bis zu den Höhen des Wahnsinns entwickelt.

Fr 25 Se Alle im Rausch erzeugt.

Fr 25 Se ... man wünscht sich ja auch ein Schwein, kein Kind.

Fr 45 Se Der KRIEG ist das eigentliche DRITTE Geschlecht.

Fr 54 Se (Sex and Crime) ... Sie bog einfach vom Dorfplatz ab. Direkt in das Verbrechen.

Fr 55 Se (Masochismus) Im übrigen sei die Wirtin "ein Geschöpf, das sich schlagen läßt, sich verkriecht und dann wieder herauskommt, als ob nichts gewesen wäre."

Fr 57 Se Wo die Häßlichkeit sich überall anbiedere, wie ein "sexueller Notstand".

Fr 111 Se Dieser Künstlergeschlechtsverkehr ... paradiesische Schamlosigkeit ... Zitat bis nichts als fad und großsprecherisch.

DARKNESS

Fr 5 darkness: Left and right it was black.
cold: I shivered as I boarded the train.

Fr 26 From the solitude . . . into the darkness.

Fr 31 But suddenly something horrific happened . . . to the point of eclipse . . . why . . . black snow. In darkness. . . . "It's sinister," he said. *Quote*

Fr 33 The sky blackened with mosquitoes.

Fr 35 Until the darkness makes the hopelessness clear.

Fr 40 On the stairs, while it was still dark, he showed me the lump. A lump the size of a duck's egg.

Fr 43 I went, when it was already dark . . . railwaymen's rooming houses.

Fr 61 How will I get out of the darkness? . . . The darkness reached the temper of insanity.

Fr 61 It might be enough, . . . the darkness in your own head (and darkness in relation to childhood—childhood experiences)

Fr 63 Darkness and cold.

Fr 69 It was already dark . . .

Fr 75 And vanished in the darkness of the shade of the trees.

Fr 81 Soon it is cold and then dark again.

Fr 88 In the darkness.

Fr 89 This man is reading in the darkness. Although it's dim, nearly dark.

F -1-

Fr 5 F Links und rechts war es schwarz.
K Mich fröstelte, als ich einstieg.

Fr 26 Fi Aus dem Alleinsein ... in die Finsternis.

Fr 31 Fi Plötzlich aber geschah etwas Grauenhaftes ... um einige Grade verfinsterte ... warum. ... schwarzen Schnee. In Finsternis. ... Es ist unheimlich, sagte er. Zitat

Fr 33 Fi Der Himmel verfinstert sich vor Mücken.

Fr 35 Fi Bis die Finsternis ihnen die Aussichtslosigkeit klar macht.

Fr 4o Fi Er zeigte mir auf der Treppe, als es noch finster war, seine Geschwulst. Eine Geschwulst in Enteneigröße.

Fr 43 Fi Ich ging, als es schon finster war ... Eisenbahnerübernachtungsräume.

Fr 61 Fi Wie komme ich aus der Finsternis? ... Die Finsternis erreicht Härtegrade des Wahnsinns.

Fr 61 Fi Es genügt unter Umständen, die Finsternis im eigenen Kopf - ... (und Finsternis in Verbindung mit Kindheit - Kindheitserlebnissen)

Fr 63 Fi Finsternis und Kälte.

Fr Fi 69 Es war schon finster ...

Fr 75 Fi Und verschwand in der Finsternis der Baumschatten.

Fr 81 Fi Bald ist es kalt und dann wieder finster.

Fr 88 Fi In der Finsternis.

Fr 89 Fi Dieser Mann liest in der Finsternis.
Obwohl es finster ist, beinahe finster.